The Morning Rituals

Practice The Morning Rituals by
marking 5 activities one by one.
Write what is on your mind,
what you're feeling, then write gratitude
for anything that you have appreciation
for and write what you will
accomplishment today. After that give
yourself a score for the morning. Read it
again before you go to sleep to see how
well you know yourself that day.

Spend quality time in the morning for
90 days to write in the morning journal.
It can help you feel good throughout the
entire day and can change you to become
a better person.

Malisa Salv

📅 DATE   🕐 WAKE UP

THE MORNING RITUALS

Silence   Meditation   Gratitude   Exercise   Reading

☐   ☐   ☐   ☐   ☐

THOUGHTS & INSIGHTS

I AM FEELING

GRATITUDE

✋ I am grateful for...

✋ I am grateful for...

✋ I am grateful for...

✋ I am grateful for...

✋ I am grateful for...

REFLECTIONS

🏔 I will accomplish...

🎯 I need to work on...

QUALITY AND INTENSITY

Focus And Breathing   1 — 2 — 3 — 4 — 5 — 6 — 7 — 8 — 9 — 10

👁 Visions And Emotions

Malisa Salvi

📅 DATE	🕐 WAKE UP

THE MORNING RITUALS

Silence	Meditation	Gratitude	Exercise	Reading
☐	☐	☐	☐	☐

THOUGHTS & INSIGHTS

I AM FEELING

GRATITUDE

🖐 I am grateful for...

🖐 I am grateful for...

🖐 I am grateful for...

🖐 I am grateful for...

🖐 I am grateful for...

REFLECTIONS

⛰ I will accomplish...

🎖 I need to work on...

QUALITY AND INTENSITY

	1	2	3	4	5	6	7	8	9	10
Focus And Breathing	○	○	○	○	○	○	○	○	○	○
Visions And Emotions	○	○	○	○	○	○	○	○	○	○

Malisa Salvi

THE MORNING RITUALS

Silence	Meditation	Gratitude	Exercise	Reading
☐	☐	☐	☐	☐

THOUGHTS & INSIGHTS

I AM FEELING

GRATITUDE

✋ I am grateful for...

✋ I am grateful for...

✋ I am grateful for...

✋ I am grateful for...

✋ I am grateful for...

REFLECTIONS

🏔 I will accomplish...

🔧 I need to work on...

QUALITY AND INTENSITY

🧘 Focus And Breathing   ○ — ○ — ○ — ○ — ○ — ○ — ○ — ○ — ○ — ○

     1 — 2 — 3 — 4 — 5 — 6 — 7 — 8 — 9 — 10

👁 Visions And Emotions   ○   ○   ○   ○   ○   ○   ○   ○   ○   ○

📅 DATE _____ 🕐 WAKE UP _____

THE MORNING RITUALS

Silence ☐ Meditation ☐ Gratitude ☐ Exercise ☐ Reading ☐

THOUGHTS & INSIGHTS

I AM FEELING

GRATITUDE

👋 I am grateful for...

👋 I am grateful for...

👋 I am grateful for...

👋 I am grateful for...

👋 I am grateful for...

REFLECTIONS

⛰️ I will accomplish...

🏋️ I need to work on...

QUALITY AND INTENSITY

Focus And Breathing — 1 — 2 — 3 — 4 — 5 — 6 — 7 — 8 — 9 — 10

👁️ Visions And Emotions

Malisa Salvi

📆 DATE   🕐 WAKE UP

THE MORNING RITUALS

Silence	Meditation	Gratitude	Exercise	Reading
☐	☐	☐	☐	☐

THOUGHTS & INSIGHTS

I AM FEELING

GRATITUDE

🤲 I am grateful for...

🤲 I am grateful for...

🤲 I am grateful for...

🤲 I am grateful for...

🤲 I am grateful for...

REFLECTIONS

⛰️ I will accomplish...

🧗 I need to work on...

QUALITY AND INTENSITY

	1	2	3	4	5	6	7	8	9	10
Focus And Breathing	○	○	○	○	○	○	○	○	○	○
Visions And Emotions	○	○	○	○	○	○	○	○	○	○

Malisa Salvi

THE MORNING RITUALS

Silence   Meditation   Gratitude   Exercise   Reading

☐   ☐   ☐   ☐   ☐

THOUGHTS & INSIGHTS   I AM FEELING

GRATITUDE

🖐 I am grateful for...

🖐 I am grateful for...

🖐 I am grateful for...

🖐 I am grateful for...

🖐 I am grateful for...

REFLECTIONS

⛰ I will accomplish...

🏋 I need to work on...

QUALITY AND INTENSITY

Focus And Breathing   ○ ○ ○ ○ ○ ○ ○ ○ ○ ○

1 — 2 — 3 — 4 — 5 — 6 — 7 — 8 — 9 — 10

Visions And Emotions   ○ ○ ○ ○ ○ ○ ○ ○ ○ ○

Malisa Salvi

📅 DATE	🕐 WAKE UP

THE MORNING RITUALS

Silence	Meditation	Gratitude	Exercise	Reading
☐	☐	☐	☐	☐

THOUGHTS & INSIGHTS

I AM FEELING

GRATITUDE

✋ I am grateful for...

✋ I am grateful for...

✋ I am grateful for...

✋ I am grateful for...

✋ I am grateful for...

REFLECTIONS

⛰️ I will accomplish...

🎚️ I need to work on...

QUALITY AND INTENSITY

		1	2	3	4	5	6	7	8	9	10
🧘 Focus And Breathing		○	○	○	○	○	○	○	○	○	○
👁️ Visions And Emotions		○	○	○	○	○	○	○	○	○	○

📅 DATE	🕐 WAKE UP

THE MORNING RITUALS

Silence	Meditation	Gratitude	Exercise	Reading
☐	☐	☐	☐	☐

THOUGHTS & INSIGHTS

I AM FEELING

GRATITUDE

🤲 I am grateful for...

🤲 I am grateful for...

🤲 I am grateful for...

🤲 I am grateful for...

🤲 I am grateful for...

REFLECTIONS

🏔️ I will accomplish...

🏋️ I need to work on...

QUALITY AND INTENSITY

🧘 Focus And Breathing	1 — 2 — 3 — 4 — 5 — 6 — 7 — 8 — 9 — 10
👁️ Visions And Emotions	○ ○ ○ ○ ○ ○ ○ ○ ○ ○

Malisa Salvi

📅 DATE   🕐 WAKE UP

THE MORNING RITUALS

Silence	Meditation	Gratitude	Exercise	Reading
☐	☐	☐	☐	☐

THOUGHTS & INSIGHTS

I AM FEELING

GRATITUDE

🖐 I am grateful for...

🖐 I am grateful for...

🖐 I am grateful for...

🖐 I am grateful for...

🖐 I am grateful for...

REFLECTIONS

🏔 I will accomplish...

👥 I need to work on...

QUALITY AND INTENSITY

👤 Focus And Breathing	
	1 — 2 — 3 — 4 — 5 — 6 — 7 — 8 — 9 — 10
👁 Visions And Emotions	

Malisa Salvi

📅 DATE   🕐 WAKE UP

THE MORNING RITUALS

Silence	Meditation	Gratitude	Exercise	Reading
☐	☐	☐	☐	☐

THOUGHTS & INSIGHTS

I AM FEELING

GRATITUDE

🖐 I am grateful for...

🖐 I am grateful for...

🖐 I am grateful for...

🖐 I am grateful for...

🖐 I am grateful for...

REFLECTIONS

⛰️ I will accomplish...

🏙️ I need to work on...

QUALITY AND INTENSITY

Focus And Breathing   1 — 2 — 3 — 4 — 5 — 6 — 7 — 8 — 9 — 10

👁 Visions And Emotions

Malisa Salvi

📅 DATE   🕐 WAKE UP

THE MORNING RITUALS

Silence	Meditation	Gratitude	Exercise	Reading
☐	☐	☐	☐	☐

THOUGHTS & INSIGHTS

I AM FEELING

GRATITUDE

🖐 I am grateful for...

🖐 I am grateful for...

🖐 I am grateful for...

🖐 I am grateful for...

🖐 I am grateful for...

REFLECTIONS

⛰ I will accomplish...

⚙ I need to work on...

QUALITY AND INTENSITY

Focus And Breathing   1 — 2 — 3 — 4 — 5 — 6 — 7 — 8 — 9 — 10

Visions And Emotions

THE MORNING RITUALS

Silence   Meditation   Gratitude   Exercise   Reading

☐   ☐   ☐   ☐   ☐

THOUGHTS & INSIGHTS

I AM FEELING

GRATITUDE

🕯 I am grateful for...

🕯 I am grateful for...

🕯 I am grateful for...

🕯 I am grateful for...

🕯 I am grateful for...

REFLECTIONS

⛰ I will accomplish...

🏋 I need to work on...

QUALITY AND INTENSITY

Focus And Breathing   1 — 2 — 3 — 4 — 5 — 6 — 7 — 8 — 9 — 10

Visions And Emotions

Malisa Salvi

📅 DATE   🕐 WAKE UP

THE MORNING RITUALS

Silence   Meditation   Gratitude   Exercise   Reading

☐   ☐   ☐   ☐   ☐

THOUGHTS & INSIGHTS

I AM FEELING

GRATITUDE

🖐 I am grateful for...

🖐 I am grateful for...

🖐 I am grateful for...

🖐 I am grateful for...

🖐 I am grateful for...

REFLECTIONS

⛰ I will accomplish...

🎯 I need to work on...

QUALITY AND INTENSITY

🧘 Focus And Breathing   1 — 2 — 3 — 4 — 5 — 6 — 7 — 8 — 9 — 10

👁 Visions And Emotions   ○ ○ ○ ○ ○ ○ ○ ○ ○ ○

📅 DATE   🕐 WAKE UP

THE MORNING RITUALS

Silence   Meditation   Gratitude   Exercise   Reading

☐   ☐   ☐   ☐   ☐

THOUGHTS & INSIGHTS

I AM FEELING

GRATITUDE

👐 I am grateful for...

👐 I am grateful for...

👐 I am grateful for...

👐 I am grateful for...

👐 I am grateful for...

REFLECTIONS

⛰️ I will accomplish...

🏋️ I need to work on...

QUALITY AND INTENSITY

	1	2	3	4	5	6	7	8	9	10
🧘 Focus And Breathing	○	○	○	○	○	○	○	○	○	○
👁️ Visions And Emotions	○	○	○	○	○	○	○	○	○	○

Malisa Salv c

📅 **DATE**   🕐 **WAKE UP**

THE MORNING RITUALS

Silence   Meditation   Gratitude   Exercise   Reading

☐   ☐   ☐   ☐   ☐

THOUGHTS & INSIGHTS

I AM FEELING

GRATITUDE

🖐 I am grateful for...

🖐 I am grateful for...

🖐 I am grateful for...

🖐 I am grateful for...

🖐 I am grateful for...

REFLECTIONS

🏔 I will accomplish...

🎯 I need to work on...

QUALITY AND INTENSITY

Focus And Breathing

1 — 2 — 3 — 4 — 5 — 6 — 7 — 8 — 9 — 10

Visions And Emotions

📅 DATE   🕐 WAKE UP

THE MORNING RITUALS

Silence   Meditation   Gratitude   Exercise   Reading

☐   ☐   ☐   ☐   ☐

THOUGHTS & INSIGHTS

I AM FEELING

GRATITUDE

✋ I am grateful for...

✋ I am grateful for...

✋ I am grateful for...

✋ I am grateful for...

✋ I am grateful for...

REFLECTIONS

⛰️ I will accomplish...

⚙️ I need to work on...

QUALITY AND INTENSITY

Focus And Breathing   1 — 2 — 3 — 4 — 5 — 6 — 7 — 8 — 9 — 10

Visions And Emotions

THE MORNING RITUALS

Silence	Meditation	Gratitude	Exercise	Reading
☐	☐	☐	☐	☐

THOUGHTS & INSIGHTS

I AM FEELING

GRATITUDE

🙏 I am grateful for...

🙏 I am grateful for...

🙏 I am grateful for...

🙏 I am grateful for...

🙏 I am grateful for...

REFLECTIONS

⛰️ I will accomplish...

🎯 I need to work on...

QUALITY AND INTENSITY

	1	2	3	4	5	6	7	8	9	10
Focus And Breathing	○	○	○	○	○	○	○	○	○	○
Visions And Emotions	○	○	○	○	○	○	○	○	○	○

THE MORNING RITUALS

Silence	Meditation	Gratitude	Exercise	Reading
☐	☐	☐	☐	☐

THOUGHTS & INSIGHTS

I AM FEELING

GRATITUDE

🖐 I am grateful for...

🖐 I am grateful for...

🖐 I am grateful for...

🖐 I am grateful for...

🖐 I am grateful for...

REFLECTIONS

⛰ I will accomplish...

📊 I need to work on...

QUALITY AND INTENSITY

Focus And Breathing   1 — 2 — 3 — 4 — 5 — 6 — 7 — 8 — 9 — 10

Visions And Emotions

THE MORNING RITUALS

Silence   Meditation   Gratitude   Exercise   Reading

☐   ☐   ☐   ☐   ☐

THOUGHTS & INSIGHTS

I AM FEELING

GRATITUDE

✋ I am grateful for...

✋ I am grateful for...

✋ I am grateful for...

✋ I am grateful for...

✋ I am grateful for...

REFLECTIONS

⛰️ I will accomplish...

🎯 I need to work on...

QUALITY AND INTENSITY

Focus And Breathing   1 — 2 — 3 — 4 — 5 — 6 — 7 — 8 — 9 — 10

👁 Visions And Emotions

Malisa Salvi

DATE   WAKE UP

THE MORNING RITUALS

Silence	Meditation	Gratitude	Exercise	Reading
☐	☐	☐	☐	☐

THOUGHTS & INSIGHTS

I AM FEELING

GRATITUDE

🖐 I am grateful for...

🖐 I am grateful for...

🖐 I am grateful for...

🖐 I am grateful for...

🖐 I am grateful for...

REFLECTIONS

⛰ I will accomplish...

🏋 I need to work on...

QUALITY AND INTENSITY

	1	2	3	4	5	6	7	8	9	10
Focus And Breathing	○	○	○	○	○	○	○	○	○	○
Visions And Emotions	○	○	○	○	○	○	○	○	○	○

Malisa Salvi

📅 DATE	🕐 WAKE UP

THE MORNING RITUALS

Silence	Meditation	Gratitude	Exercise	Reading
☐	☐	☐	☐	☐

THOUGHTS & INSIGHTS

I AM FEELING

GRATITUDE

🖐 I am grateful for...

🖐 I am grateful for...

🖐 I am grateful for...

🖐 I am grateful for...

🖐 I am grateful for...

REFLECTIONS

⛰ I will accomplish...

🏋 I need to work on...

QUALITY AND INTENSITY

	1	2	3	4	5	6	7	8	9	10
Focus And Breathing										
Visions And Emotions										

📅 DATE   🕐 WAKE UP

THE MORNING RITUALS

Silence   Meditation   Gratitude   Exercise   Reading
☐   ☐   ☐   ☐   ☐

THOUGHTS & INSIGHTS

I AM FEELING

GRATITUDE

👐 I am grateful for...

👐 I am grateful for...

👐 I am grateful for...

👐 I am grateful for...

👐 I am grateful for...

REFLECTIONS

⛰️ I will accomplish...

⚙️ I need to work on...

QUALITY AND INTENSITY

👁️‍🗨️ Focus And Breathing   1 — 2 — 3 — 4 — 5 — 6 — 7 — 8 — 9 — 10

👁️ Visions And Emotions

Malisa Salvi

📅 DATE   🕐 WAKE UP

THE MORNING RITUALS

Silence	Meditation	Gratitude	Exercise	Reading
☐	☐	☐	☐	☐

THOUGHTS & INSIGHTS

I AM FEELING

GRATITUDE

✋ I am grateful for...

✋ I am grateful for...

✋ I am grateful for...

✋ I am grateful for...

✋ I am grateful for...

REFLECTIONS

🏔️ I will accomplish...

🎚️ I need to work on...

QUALITY AND INTENSITY

👤 Focus And Breathing

1 — 2 — 3 — 4 — 5 — 6 — 7 — 8 — 9 — 10

👁️ Visions And Emotions

Malisa Salvi

📅 DATE   🕐 WAKE UP

THE MORNING RITUALS

Silence   Meditation   Gratitude   Exercise   Reading

☐   ☐   ☐   ☐   ☐

THOUGHTS & INSIGHTS

I AM FEELING

GRATITUDE

👐 I am grateful for...

👐 I am grateful for...

👐 I am grateful for...

👐 I am grateful for...

👐 I am grateful for...

REFLECTIONS

⛰️ I will accomplish...

🏋️ I need to work on...

QUALITY AND INTENSITY

Focus And Breathing   1 — 2 — 3 — 4 — 5 — 6 — 7 — 8 — 9 — 10

Visions And Emotions

Malisa Salvi

THE MORNING RITUALS

Silence   Meditation   Gratitude   Exercise   Reading

☐   ☐   ☐   ☐   ☐

THOUGHTS & INSIGHTS

I AM FEELING

GRATITUDE

🤲 I am grateful for...

🤲 I am grateful for...

🤲 I am grateful for...

🤲 I am grateful for...

🤲 I am grateful for...

REFLECTIONS

⛰️ I will accomplish...

🎯 I need to work on...

QUALITY AND INTENSITY

Focus And Breathing   1 — 2 — 3 — 4 — 5 — 6 — 7 — 8 — 9 — 10

Visions And Emotions

Malisa Salvi

THE MORNING RITUALS

Silence	Meditation	Gratitude	Exercise	Reading
☐	☐	☐	☐	☐

THOUGHTS & INSIGHTS

I AM FEELING

GRATITUDE

🖐 I am grateful for...

🖐 I am grateful for...

🖐 I am grateful for...

🖐 I am grateful for...

🖐 I am grateful for...

REFLECTIONS

⛰ I will accomplish...

🏋 I need to work on...

QUALITY AND INTENSITY

Focus And Breathing   1 — 2 — 3 — 4 — 5 — 6 — 7 — 8 — 9 — 10

👁 Visions And Emotions

Malisa Salvi

📓 DATE	🕐 WAKE UP

THE MORNING RITUALS

Silence	Meditation	Gratitude	Exercise	Reading
☐	☐	☐	☐	☐

THOUGHTS & INSIGHTS

I AM FEELING

GRATITUDE

✋ I am grateful for...

✋ I am grateful for...

✋ I am grateful for...

✋ I am grateful for...

✋ I am grateful for...

REFLECTIONS

🏔 I will accomplish...

🏘 I need to work on...

QUALITY AND INTENSITY

| 🧘 Focus And Breathing | 1 — 2 — 3 — 4 — 5 — 6 — 7 — 8 — 9 — 10 |
| 👁 Visions And Emotions | |

Malisa Salvi

📅 DATE   🕐 WAKE UP

THE MORNING RITUALS

Silence	Meditation	Gratitude	Exercise	Reading
☐	☐	☐	☐	☐

THOUGHTS & INSIGHTS

I AM FEELING

GRATITUDE

✍ I am grateful for...

✍ I am grateful for...

✍ I am grateful for...

✍ I am grateful for...

✍ I am grateful for...

REFLECTIONS

⛰ I will accomplish...

🏋 I need to work on...

QUALITY AND INTENSITY

Focus And Breathing   1 — 2 — 3 — 4 — 5 — 6 — 7 — 8 — 9 — 10

Visions And Emotions   ○   ○   ○   ○   ○   ○   ○   ○   ○   ○

📅 DATE　　　　　　　🕐 WAKE UP

THE MORNING RITUALS

Silence　　　Meditation　　　Gratitude　　　Exercise　　　Reading

☐　　　　　☐　　　　　☐　　　　　☐　　　　　☐

THOUGHTS & INSIGHTS

I AM FEELING

GRATITUDE

🖐 I am grateful for...

🖐 I am grateful for...

🖐 I am grateful for...

🖐 I am grateful for...

🖐 I am grateful for...

REFLECTIONS

⛰ I will accomplish...

🏋 I need to work on...

QUALITY AND INTENSITY

Focus And Breathing　　1 — 2 — 3 — 4 — 5 — 6 — 7 — 8 — 9 — 10

👁 Visions And Emotions　○　○　○　○　○　○　○　○　○　○

Malisa Salvi

📅 DATE   🕐 WAKE UP

THE MORNING RITUALS

Silence   Meditation   Gratitude   Exercise   Reading

☐   ☐   ☐   ☐   ☐

THOUGHTS & INSIGHTS

I AM FEELING

GRATITUDE

🖐 I am grateful for...

🖐 I am grateful for...

🖐 I am grateful for...

🖐 I am grateful for...

🖐 I am grateful for...

REFLECTIONS

⛰ I will accomplish...

📊 I need to work on...

QUALITY AND INTENSITY

Focus And Breathing   1 — 2 — 3 — 4 — 5 — 6 — 7 — 8 — 9 — 10

👁 Visions And Emotions

Malisa Salve

📅 DATE   🕐 WAKE UP

THE MORNING RITUALS

Silence	Meditation	Gratitude	Exercise	Reading
☐	☐	☐	☐	☐

THOUGHTS & INSIGHTS

I AM FEELING

GRATITUDE

✋ I am grateful for...

✋ I am grateful for...

✋ I am grateful for...

✋ I am grateful for...

✋ I am grateful for...

REFLECTIONS

⛰️ I will accomplish...

🏗️ I need to work on...

QUALITY AND INTENSITY

Focus And Breathing   1 — 2 — 3 — 4 — 5 — 6 — 7 — 8 — 9 — 10

👁️ Visions And Emotions   ○ ○ ○ ○ ○ ○ ○ ○ ○ ○

Malisa Salvi

THE MORNING RITUALS

Silence　　Meditation　　Gratitude　　Exercise　　Reading
☐　　　　☐　　　　☐　　　　☐　　　　☐

THOUGHTS & INSIGHTS

I AM FEELING

GRATITUDE

🤲 I am grateful for...

🤲 I am grateful for...

🤲 I am grateful for...

🤲 I am grateful for...

🤲 I am grateful for...

REFLECTIONS

⛰️ I will accomplish...

🏋️ I need to work on...

QUALITY AND INTENSITY

Focus And Breathing ⭘ ⭘ ⭘ ⭘ ⭘ ⭘ ⭘ ⭘ ⭘ ⭘
1 — 2 — 3 — 4 — 5 — 6 — 7 — 8 — 9 — 10
👁️ Visions And Emotions ⭘ ⭘ ⭘ ⭘ ⭘ ⭘ ⭘ ⭘ ⭘ ⭘

Malisa Salvi

THE MORNING RITUALS

Silence	Meditation	Gratitude	Exercise	Reading
☐	☐	☐	☐	☐

THOUGHTS & INSIGHTS

I AM FEELING

GRATITUDE

✍ I am grateful for...

✍ I am grateful for...

✍ I am grateful for...

✍ I am grateful for...

✍ I am grateful for...

REFLECTIONS

🏔 I will accomplish...

⚙ I need to work on...

QUALITY AND INTENSITY

	1	2	3	4	5	6	7	8	9	10
Focus And Breathing										
Visions And Emotions										

Malisa Salvi

DATE

WAKE UP

THE MORNING RITUALS

Silence	Meditation	Gratitude	Exercise	Reading
☐	☐	☐	☐	☐

THOUGHTS & INSIGHTS

I AM FEELING

GRATITUDE

✋ I am grateful for...

✋ I am grateful for...

✋ I am grateful for...

✋ I am grateful for...

✋ I am grateful for...

REFLECTIONS

🏔️ I will accomplish...

📊 I need to work on...

QUALITY AND INTENSITY

	Focus And Breathing	1 — 2 — 3 — 4 — 5 — 6 — 7 — 8 — 9 — 10
👁	Visions And Emotions	

DATE   WAKE UP

THE MORNING RITUALS

Silence   Meditation   Gratitude   Exercise   Reading

☐   ☐   ☐   ☐   ☐

THOUGHTS & INSIGHTS

I AM FEELING

GRATITUDE

🖐 I am grateful for...

🖐 I am grateful for...

🖐 I am grateful for...

🖐 I am grateful for...

🖐 I am grateful for...

REFLECTIONS

🏔 I will accomplish...

🏋 I need to work on...

QUALITY AND INTENSITY

Focus And Breathing   1 — 2 — 3 — 4 — 5 — 6 — 7 — 8 — 9 — 10

Visions And Emotions   ○ ○ ○ ○ ○ ○ ○ ○ ○ ○

Malisa Salvi

📅 DATE	🕐 WAKE UP

THE MORNING RITUALS

Silence	Meditation	Gratitude	Exercise	Reading
☐	☐	☐	☐	☐

THOUGHTS & INSIGHTS

I AM FEELING

GRATITUDE

🖐 I am grateful for...

🖐 I am grateful for...

🖐 I am grateful for...

🖐 I am grateful for...

🖐 I am grateful for...

REFLECTIONS

🏔 I will accomplish...

🏋 I need to work on...

QUALITY AND INTENSITY

Focus And Breathing   1 — 2 — 3 — 4 — 5 — 6 — 7 — 8 — 9 — 10

👁 Visions And Emotions

Malisa Salvi

📅 **DATE**   🕐 **WAKE UP**

THE MORNING RITUALS

Silence	Meditation	Gratitude	Exercise	Reading
☐	☐	☐	☐	☐

THOUGHTS & INSIGHTS

I AM FEELING

GRATITUDE

✍ I am grateful for...

✍ I am grateful for...

✍ I am grateful for...

✍ I am grateful for...

✍ I am grateful for...

REFLECTIONS

⛰ I will accomplish...

🏋 I need to work on...

QUALITY AND INTENSITY

	1	2	3	4	5	6	7	8	9	10
👤 Focus And Breathing	○	○	○	○	○	○	○	○	○	○
👁 Visions And Emotions	○	○	○	○	○	○	○	○	○	○

Malisa Salvi

📅 DATE   🕐 WAKE UP

THE MORNING RITUALS

Silence   Meditation   Gratitude   Exercise   Reading

☐   ☐   ☐   ☐   ☐

THOUGHTS & INSIGHTS

I AM FEELING

GRATITUDE

✋ I am grateful for...

✋ I am grateful for...

✋ I am grateful for...

✋ I am grateful for...

✋ I am grateful for...

REFLECTIONS

⛰️ I will accomplish...

📈 I need to work on...

QUALITY AND INTENSITY

🧘 Focus And Breathing   1 — 2 — 3 — 4 — 5 — 6 — 7 — 8 — 9 — 10

👁️ Visions And Emotions   ○ ○ ○ ○ ○ ○ ○ ○ ○ ○

Malisa Salvi

THE MORNING RITUALS

Silence   Meditation   Gratitude   Exercise   Reading

☐   ☐   ☐   ☐   ☐

THOUGHTS & INSIGHTS

I AM FEELING

GRATITUDE

✍ I am grateful for...

✍ I am grateful for...

✍ I am grateful for...

✍ I am grateful for...

✍ I am grateful for...

REFLECTIONS

⛰ I will accomplish...

🏰 I need to work on...

QUALITY AND INTENSITY

Focus And Breathing   ○—1—○—2—○—3—○—4—○—5—○—6—○—7—○—8—○—9—○—10

👁 Visions And Emotions   ○ ○ ○ ○ ○ ○ ○ ○ ○ ○

DATE

WAKE UP

THE MORNING RITUALS

Silence ☐   Meditation ☐   Gratitude ☐   Exercise ☐   Reading ☐

THOUGHTS & INSIGHTS

I AM FEELING

GRATITUDE

👏 I am grateful for...

👏 I am grateful for...

👏 I am grateful for...

👏 I am grateful for...

👏 I am grateful for...

REFLECTIONS

⛰️ I will accomplish...

⚙️ I need to work on...

QUALITY AND INTENSITY

Focus And Breathing

Visions And Emotions

1 — 2 — 3 — 4 — 5 — 6 — 7 — 8 — 9 — 10

Malisa Salvi

| 📅 DATE | 🕐 WAKE UP |

THE MORNING RITUALS

Silence	Meditation	Gratitude	Exercise	Reading
☐	☐	☐	☐	☐

THOUGHTS & INSIGHTS

I AM FEELING

GRATITUDE

🖐 I am grateful for...

🖐 I am grateful for...

🖐 I am grateful for...

🖐 I am grateful for...

🖐 I am grateful for...

REFLECTIONS

⛰ I will accomplish...

🎖 I need to work on...

QUALITY AND INTENSITY

	1	2	3	4	5	6	7	8	9	10
Focus And Breathing	○	○	○	○	○	○	○	○	○	○
Visions And Emotions	○	○	○	○	○	○	○	○	○	○

Malisa Salvi

📅 DATE   🕐 WAKE UP

THE MORNING RITUALS

Silence   Meditation   Gratitude   Exercise   Reading

☐   ☐   ☐   ☐   ☐

THOUGHTS & INSIGHTS

I AM FEELING

GRATITUDE

🤲 I am grateful for...

🤲 I am grateful for...

🤲 I am grateful for...

🤲 I am grateful for...

🤲 I am grateful for...

REFLECTIONS

⛰️ I will accomplish...

🏆 I need to work on...

QUALITY AND INTENSITY

Focus And Breathing   1 — 2 — 3 — 4 — 5 — 6 — 7 — 8 — 9 — 10

Visions And Emotions

Malisa Salvi

📅 DATE   🕐 WAKE UP

THE MORNING RITUALS

Silence	Meditation	Gratitude	Exercise	Reading
☐	☐	☐	☐	☐

THOUGHTS & INSIGHTS

I AM FEELING

GRATITUDE

✍ I am grateful for...

✍ I am grateful for...

✍ I am grateful for...

✍ I am grateful for...

✍ I am grateful for...

REFLECTIONS

🏔 I will accomplish...

⚙ I need to work on...

QUALITY AND INTENSITY

🧘 Focus And Breathing   1 — 2 — 3 — 4 — 5 — 6 — 7 — 8 — 9 — 10

👁 Visions And Emotions

Malisa Salvi

📅 DATE	🕐 WAKE UP

THE MORNING RITUALS

Silence	Meditation	Gratitude	Exercise	Reading
☐	☐	☐	☐	☐

THOUGHTS & INSIGHTS

I AM FEELING

GRATITUDE

✋ I am grateful for...

✋ I am grateful for...

✋ I am grateful for...

✋ I am grateful for...

✋ I am grateful for...

REFLECTIONS

🏔️ I will accomplish...

🎯 I need to work on...

QUALITY AND INTENSITY

		1	2	3	4	5	6	7	8	9	10
🧘 Focus And Breathing		○	○	○	○	○	○	○	○	○	○
👁 Visions And Emotions		○	○	○	○	○	○	○	○	○	○

Malisa Salv

THE MORNING RITUALS

Silence   Meditation   Gratitude   Exercise   Reading

☐   ☐   ☐   ☐   ☐

THOUGHTS & INSIGHTS

I AM FEELING

GRATITUDE

🖐 I am grateful for...

🖐 I am grateful for...

🖐 I am grateful for...

🖐 I am grateful for...

🖐 I am grateful for...

REFLECTIONS

🏔 I will accomplish...

🏋 I need to work on...

QUALITY AND INTENSITY

Focus And Breathing   1 — 2 — 3 — 4 — 5 — 6 — 7 — 8 — 9 — 10

👁 Visions And Emotions

📅 DATE	🕐 WAKE UP

THE MORNING RITUALS

Silence	Meditation	Gratitude	Exercise	Reading
☐	☐	☐	☐	☐

THOUGHTS & INSIGHTS

I AM FEELING

GRATITUDE

🖐 I am grateful for...

🖐 I am grateful for...

🖐 I am grateful for...

🖐 I am grateful for...

🖐 I am grateful for...

REFLECTIONS

🏔 I will accomplish...

🏙 I need to work on...

QUALITY AND INTENSITY

Focus And Breathing   1 — 2 — 3 — 4 — 5 — 6 — 7 — 8 — 9 — 10

👁 Visions And Emotions   1 2 3 4 5 6 7 8 9 10

Malisa Galvi

📅 DATE   🕐 WAKE UP

THE MORNING RITUALS

Silence	Meditation	Gratitude	Exercise	Reading
☐	☐	☐	☐	☐

THOUGHTS & INSIGHTS

I AM FEELING

GRATITUDE

🖐 I am grateful for…

🖐 I am grateful for…

🖐 I am grateful for…

🖐 I am grateful for…

🖐 I am grateful for…

REFLECTIONS

⛰ I will accomplish…

I need to work on…

QUALITY AND INTENSITY

Focus And Breathing   1 — 2 — 3 — 4 — 5 — 6 — 7 — 8 — 9 — 10

Visions And Emotions   ○ ○ ○ ○ ○ ○ ○ ○ ○ ○

📅 DATE   🕐 WAKE UP

THE MORNING RITUALS

Silence   Meditation   Gratitude   Exercise   Reading
☐   ☐   ☐   ☐   ☐

THOUGHTS & INSIGHTS   ## I AM FEELING

GRATITUDE

✍ I am grateful for...

✍ I am grateful for...

✍ I am grateful for...

✍ I am grateful for...

✍ I am grateful for...

REFLECTIONS

🏔 I will accomplish...

🎯 I need to work on...

QUALITY AND INTENSITY

📖 Focus And Breathing   ○ — ○ — ○ — ○ — ○ — ○ — ○ — ○ — ○ — ○
                            1   2   3   4   5   6   7   8   9   10
👁 Visions And Emotions   ○   ○   ○   ○   ○   ○   ○   ○   ○   ○

Malisa Salv

THE MORNING RITUALS

Silence	Meditation	Gratitude	Exercise	Reading
☐	☐	☐	☐	☐

THOUGHTS & INSIGHTS

I AM FEELING

GRATITUDE

🖐 I am grateful for...

🖐 I am grateful for...

🖐 I am grateful for...

🖐 I am grateful for...

🖐 I am grateful for...

REFLECTIONS

⛰ I will accomplish...

🏋 I need to work on...

QUALITY AND INTENSITY

🧘 Focus And Breathing   1 — 2 — 3 — 4 — 5 — 6 — 7 — 8 — 9 — 10

👁 Visions And Emotions   ○ ○ ○ ○ ○ ○ ○ ○ ○ ○

Malisa Salvi

📅 DATE   🕐 WAKE UP

THE MORNING RITUALS

Silence   Meditation   Gratitude   Exercise   Reading
☐   ☐   ☐   ☐   ☐

THOUGHTS & INSIGHTS

I AM FEELING

GRATITUDE

✋ I am grateful for...

✋ I am grateful for...

✋ I am grateful for...

✋ I am grateful for...

✋ I am grateful for...

REFLECTIONS

🏔 I will accomplish...

⚙ I need to work on...

QUALITY AND INTENSITY

	1	2	3	4	5	6	7	8	9	10
👤 Focus And Breathing	○	○	○	○	○	○	○	○	○	○
👁 Visions And Emotions	○	○	○	○	○	○	○	○	○	○

Malisa Salvi

📅 DATE   🕐 WAKE UP

THE MORNING RITUALS

Silence   Meditation   Gratitude   Exercise   Reading
☐   ☐   ☐   ☐   ☐

THOUGHTS & INSIGHTS

I AM FEELING

GRATITUDE

✋ I am grateful for...

✋ I am grateful for...

✋ I am grateful for...

✋ I am grateful for...

✋ I am grateful for...

REFLECTIONS

🏔 I will accomplish...

🎯 I need to work on...

QUALITY AND INTENSITY

	1	2	3	4	5	6	7	8	9	10
Focus And Breathing	○	○	○	○	○	○	○	○	○	○
Visions And Emotions	○	○	○	○	○	○	○	○	○	○

📅 DATE ⏰ WAKE UP

THE MORNING RITUALS

Silence   Meditation   Gratitude   Exercise   Reading
☐   ☐   ☐   ☐   ☐

THOUGHTS & INSIGHTS

I AM FEELING

GRATITUDE

🖐 I am grateful for...

🖐 I am grateful for...

🖐 I am grateful for...

🖐 I am grateful for...

🖐 I am grateful for...

REFLECTIONS

⛰ I will accomplish...

⚙ I need to work on...

QUALITY AND INTENSITY

Focus And Breathing   ○ ── ○ ── ○ ── ○ ── ○ ── ○ ── ○ ── ○ ── ○ ── ○
                           1 ── 2 ── 3 ── 4 ── 5 ── 6 ── 7 ── 8 ── 9 ──10

👁 Visions And Emotions   ○   ○   ○   ○   ○   ○   ○   ○   ○   ○

THE MORNING RITUALS

Silence	Meditation	Gratitude	Exercise	Reading
☐	☐	☐	☐	☐

THOUGHTS & INSIGHTS

I AM FEELING

GRATITUDE

🙌 I am grateful for...

🙌 I am grateful for...

🙌 I am grateful for...

🙌 I am grateful for...

🙌 I am grateful for...

REFLECTIONS

⛰️ I will accomplish...

🏋️ I need to work on...

QUALITY AND INTENSITY

Focus And Breathing   1 — 2 — 3 — 4 — 5 — 6 — 7 — 8 — 9 — 10

Visions And Emotions

📅 DATE   🕐 WAKE UP

THE MORNING RITUALS

Silence	Meditation	Gratitude	Exercise	Reading
☐	☐	☐	☐	☐

THOUGHTS & INSIGHTS

I AM FEELING

GRATITUDE

🖐 I am grateful for…

🖐 I am grateful for…

🖐 I am grateful for…

🖐 I am grateful for…

🖐 I am grateful for…

REFLECTIONS

⛰️ I will accomplish…

🏋️ I need to work on…

QUALITY AND INTENSITY

	1	2	3	4	5	6	7	8	9	10
Focus And Breathing	○	○	○	○	○	○	○	○	○	○
Visions And Emotions	○	○	○	○	○	○	○	○	○	○

Malisa Salvi

📅 DATE	🕐 WAKE UP

THE MORNING RITUALS

Silence	Meditation	Gratitude	Exercise	Reading
☐	☐	☐	☐	☐

THOUGHTS & INSIGHTS

I AM FEELING

GRATITUDE

✋ I am grateful for...

✋ I am grateful for...

✋ I am grateful for...

✋ I am grateful for...

✋ I am grateful for...

REFLECTIONS

⛰️ I will accomplish...

🏋️ I need to work on...

QUALITY AND INTENSITY

🧘 Focus And Breathing										
	1	2	3	4	5	6	7	8	9	10
👁️ Visions And Emotions										

Malisa Salvi

📅 DATE	🕐 WAKE UP

THE MORNING RITUALS

Silence	Meditation	Gratitude	Exercise	Reading
☐	☐	☐	☐	☐

THOUGHTS & INSIGHTS

I AM FEELING

GRATITUDE

👋 I am grateful for...

👋 I am grateful for...

👋 I am grateful for...

👋 I am grateful for...

👋 I am grateful for...

REFLECTIONS

🏔 I will accomplish...

🚶 I need to work on...

QUALITY AND INTENSITY

	1	2	3	4	5	6	7	8	9	10
Focus And Breathing	○	○	○	○	○	○	○	○	○	○
Visions And Emotions	○	○	○	○	○	○	○	○	○	○

Malisa Salvi

📅 DATE	🕐 WAKE UP

THE MORNING RITUALS

Silence	Meditation	Gratitude	Exercise	Reading
☐	☐	☐	☐	☐

THOUGHTS & INSIGHTS

I AM FEELING

GRATITUDE

✋ I am grateful for...

✋ I am grateful for...

✋ I am grateful for...

✋ I am grateful for...

✋ I am grateful for...

REFLECTIONS

🏔 I will accomplish...

🏛 I need to work on...

QUALITY AND INTENSITY

	1	2	3	4	5	6	7	8	9	10
👤 Focus And Breathing	○	○	○	○	○	○	○	○	○	○
👁 Visions And Emotions	○	○	○	○	○	○	○	○	○	○

📅 DATE   🕐 WAKE UP

THE MORNING RITUALS

Silence	Meditation	Gratitude	Exercise	Reading
☐	☐	☐	☐	☐

THOUGHTS & INSIGHTS

I AM FEELING

GRATITUDE

🙏 I am grateful for...

🙏 I am grateful for...

🙏 I am grateful for...

🙏 I am grateful for...

🙏 I am grateful for...

REFLECTIONS

🏔️ I will accomplish...

🏋️ I need to work on...

QUALITY AND INTENSITY

	1	2	3	4	5	6	7	8	9	10
Focus And Breathing										
Visions And Emotions										

THE MORNING RITUALS

Silence	Meditation	Gratitude	Exercise	Reading
☐	☐	☐	☐	☐

THOUGHTS & INSIGHTS

I AM FEELING

GRATITUDE

✋ I am grateful for...

✋ I am grateful for...

✋ I am grateful for...

✋ I am grateful for...

✋ I am grateful for...

REFLECTIONS

⛰️ I will accomplish...

I need to work on...

QUALITY AND INTENSITY

Focus And Breathing   1 — 2 — 3 — 4 — 5 — 6 — 7 — 8 — 9 — 10

👁️ Visions And Emotions

📅 DATE   🕐 WAKE UP

THE MORNING RITUALS

Silence   Meditation   Gratitude   Exercise   Reading

☐   ☐   ☐   ☐   ☐

THOUGHTS & INSIGHTS

I AM FEELING

GRATITUDE

🖐 I am grateful for...

🖐 I am grateful for...

🖐 I am grateful for...

🖐 I am grateful for...

🖐 I am grateful for...

REFLECTIONS

🏔 I will accomplish...

🏋 I need to work on...

QUALITY AND INTENSITY

🧘 Focus And Breathing   ○ ○ ○ ○ ○ ○ ○ ○ ○ ○

      1 — 2 — 3 — 4 — 5 — 6 — 7 — 8 — 9 — 10

👁 Visions And Emotions   ○ ○ ○ ○ ○ ○ ○ ○ ○ ○

Malissa Salvi

📅 DATE   🕐 WAKE UP

THE MORNING RITUALS

Silence	Meditation	Gratitude	Exercise	Reading
☐	☐	☐	☐	☐

THOUGHTS & INSIGHTS

I AM FEELING

GRATITUDE

✍ I am grateful for...

✍ I am grateful for...

✍ I am grateful for...

✍ I am grateful for...

✍ I am grateful for...

REFLECTIONS

⛰ I will accomplish...

🏗 I need to work on...

QUALITY AND INTENSITY

	1	2	3	4	5	6	7	8	9	10
Focus And Breathing										
Visions And Emotions										

THE MORNING RITUALS

Silence   Meditation   Gratitude   Exercise   Reading

☐   ☐   ☐   ☐   ☐

THOUGHTS & INSIGHTS

I AM FEELING

GRATITUDE

✋ I am grateful for...

✋ I am grateful for...

✋ I am grateful for...

✋ I am grateful for...

✋ I am grateful for...

REFLECTIONS

⛰️ I will accomplish...

🏋️ I need to work on...

QUALITY AND INTENSITY

	1	2	3	4	5	6	7	8	9	10
🧘 Focus And Breathing	○	○	○	○	○	○	○	○	○	○
👁️ Visions And Emotions	○	○	○	○	○	○	○	○	○	○

Malisa Salvi

THE MORNING RITUALS

Silence	Meditation	Gratitude	Exercise	Reading
☐	☐	☐	☐	☐

THOUGHTS & INSIGHTS

I AM FEELING

GRATITUDE

✋ I am grateful for...

✋ I am grateful for...

✋ I am grateful for...

✋ I am grateful for...

✋ I am grateful for...

REFLECTIONS

🏔 I will accomplish...

🎚 I need to work on...

QUALITY AND INTENSITY

Focus And Breathing

1 — 2 — 3 — 4 — 5 — 6 — 7 — 8 — 9 — 10

Visions And Emotions

📅 DATE	🕐 WAKE UP

THE MORNING RITUALS

Silence	Meditation	Gratitude	Exercise	Reading
☐	☐	☐	☐	☐

THOUGHTS & INSIGHTS

I AM FEELING

GRATITUDE

🖐 I am grateful for...

🖐 I am grateful for...

🖐 I am grateful for...

🖐 I am grateful for...

🖐 I am grateful for...

REFLECTIONS

⛰ I will accomplish...

⚙ I need to work on...

QUALITY AND INTENSITY

		1	2	3	4	5	6	7	8	9	10
🧘 Focus And Breathing		○	○	○	○	○	○	○	○	○	○
👁 Visions And Emotions		○	○	○	○	○	○	○	○	○	○

Malisa Salvi

THE MORNING RITUALS

Silence	Meditation	Gratitude	Exercise	Reading
☐	☐	☐	☐	☐

THOUGHTS & INSIGHTS

I AM FEELING

GRATITUDE

✋ I am grateful for...

✋ I am grateful for...

✋ I am grateful for...

✋ I am grateful for...

✋ I am grateful for...

REFLECTIONS

⛰️ I will accomplish...

🏋️ I need to work on...

QUALITY AND INTENSITY

		1	2	3	4	5	6	7	8	9	10
😤 Focus And Breathing											
👁️ Visions And Emotions											

Malisa Salve

📅 DATE	🕐 WAKE UP

THE MORNING RITUALS

Silence	Meditation	Gratitude	Exercise	Reading
☐	☐	☐	☐	☐

THOUGHTS & INSIGHTS

I AM FEELING

GRATITUDE

👋 I am grateful for...

👋 I am grateful for...

👋 I am grateful for...

👋 I am grateful for...

👋 I am grateful for...

REFLECTIONS

🏔 I will accomplish...

🎯 I need to work on...

QUALITY AND INTENSITY

Focus And Breathing	○	○	○	○	○	○	○	○	○	○
	1	2	3	4	5	6	7	8	9	10
👁 Visions And Emotions	○	○	○	○	○	○	○	○	○	○

Malisa Salvi

🗓 DATE	🕐 WAKE UP

THE MORNING RITUALS

Silence	Meditation	Gratitude	Exercise	Reading
☐	☐	☐	☐	☐

THOUGHTS & INSIGHTS

I AM FEELING

GRATITUDE

🖐 I am grateful for...

🖐 I am grateful for...

🖐 I am grateful for...

🖐 I am grateful for...

🖐 I am grateful for...

REFLECTIONS

🏔 I will accomplish...

🏛 I need to work on...

QUALITY AND INTENSITY

	Focus And Breathing	1 — 2 — 3 — 4 — 5 — 6 — 7 — 8 — 9 — 10
	Visions And Emotions	

Malisa Salvi

📅 DATE   🕐 WAKE UP

THE MORNING RITUALS

Silence   Meditation   Gratitude   Exercise   Reading

☐   ☐   ☐   ☐   ☐

THOUGHTS & INSIGHTS

I AM FEELING

GRATITUDE

👋 I am grateful for...

👋 I am grateful for...

👋 I am grateful for...

👋 I am grateful for...

👋 I am grateful for...

REFLECTIONS

🏔️ I will accomplish...

🏋️ I need to work on...

QUALITY AND INTENSITY

Focus And Breathing   ○ ○ ○ ○ ○ ○ ○ ○ ○ ○

1 — 2 — 3 — 4 — 5 — 6 — 7 — 8 — 9 — 10

👁️ Visions And Emotions   ○ ○ ○ ○ ○ ○ ○ ○ ○ ○

Malisa Salvi

📅 DATE   🕐 WAKE UP

THE MORNING RITUALS

Silence   Meditation   Gratitude   Exercise   Reading
☐   ☐   ☐   ☐   ☐

THOUGHTS & INSIGHTS

I AM FEELING

GRATITUDE

✍ I am grateful for...

✍ I am grateful for...

✍ I am grateful for...

✍ I am grateful for...

✍ I am grateful for...

REFLECTIONS

⛰ I will accomplish...

🎖 I need to work on...

QUALITY AND INTENSITY

Focus And Breathing   1 — 2 — 3 — 4 — 5 — 6 — 7 — 8 — 9 — 10

👁 Visions And Emotions

📅 DATE _____   🕐 WAKE UP _____

THE MORNING RITUALS

Silence	Meditation	Gratitude	Exercise	Reading
☐	☐	☐	☐	☐

THOUGHTS & INSIGHTS

I AM FEELING

GRATITUDE

🖐 I am grateful for...

🖐 I am grateful for...

🖐 I am grateful for...

🖐 I am grateful for...

🖐 I am grateful for...

REFLECTIONS

⛰️ I will accomplish...

⚙️ I need to work on...

QUALITY AND INTENSITY

Focus And Breathing   1 — 2 — 3 — 4 — 5 — 6 — 7 — 8 — 9 — 10

👁 Visions And Emotions   ○ ○ ○ ○ ○ ○ ○ ○ ○ ○

Malisa Salv

THE MORNING RITUALS

Silence	Meditation	Gratitude	Exercise	Reading
☐	☐	☐	☐	☐

THOUGHTS & INSIGHTS

I AM FEELING

GRATITUDE

✋ I am grateful for...

✋ I am grateful for...

✋ I am grateful for...

✋ I am grateful for...

✋ I am grateful for...

REFLECTIONS

⛰️ I will accomplish...

🎖️ I need to work on...

QUALITY AND INTENSITY

Focus And Breathing

1 — 2 — 3 — 4 — 5 — 6 — 7 — 8 — 9 — 10

👁️ Visions And Emotions

📅 DATE   🕐 WAKE UP

THE MORNING RITUALS

Silence   Meditation   Gratitude   Exercise   Reading

☐   ☐   ☐   ☐   ☐

THOUGHTS & INSIGHTS

I AM FEELING

GRATITUDE

🖐 I am grateful for...

🖐 I am grateful for...

🖐 I am grateful for...

🖐 I am grateful for...

🖐 I am grateful for...

REFLECTIONS

⛰ I will accomplish...

🎯 I need to work on...

QUALITY AND INTENSITY

🧘 Focus And Breathing   1 — 2 — 3 — 4 — 5 — 6 — 7 — 8 — 9 — 10

👁 Visions And Emotions   ○ ○ ○ ○ ○ ○ ○ ○ ○ ○

Malisa Salvi

THE MORNING RITUALS

Silence	Meditation	Gratitude	Exercise	Reading
☐	☐	☐	☐	☐

THOUGHTS & INSIGHTS

I AM FEELING

GRATITUDE

✋ I am grateful for...

✋ I am grateful for...

✋ I am grateful for...

✋ I am grateful for...

✋ I am grateful for...

REFLECTIONS

⛰️ I will accomplish...

🎖️ I need to work on...

QUALITY AND INTENSITY

Focus And Breathing	1 — 2 — 3 — 4 — 5 — 6 — 7 — 8 — 9 — 10
Visions And Emotions	○ ○ ○ ○ ○ ○ ○ ○ ○ ○

Malisa Salvi

📅 DATE	🕐 WAKE UP

THE MORNING RITUALS

Silence	Meditation	Gratitude	Exercise	Reading
☐	☐	☐	☐	☐

THOUGHTS & INSIGHTS

I AM FEELING

GRATITUDE

✋ I am grateful for...

✋ I am grateful for...

✋ I am grateful for...

✋ I am grateful for...

✋ I am grateful for...

REFLECTIONS

⛰️ I will accomplish...

🎯 I need to work on...

QUALITY AND INTENSITY

🧘 Focus And Breathing	○	○	○	○	○	○	○	○	○	○
	1 — 2 — 3 — 4 — 5 — 6 — 7 — 8 — 9 — 10									
👁️ Visions And Emotions	○	○	○	○	○	○	○	○	○	○

📆 DATE	🕐 WAKE UP

THE MORNING RITUALS

Silence	Meditation	Gratitude	Exercise	Reading
☐	☐	☐	☐	☐

THOUGHTS & INSIGHTS

I AM FEELING

GRATITUDE

✋ I am grateful for...

✋ I am grateful for...

✋ I am grateful for...

✋ I am grateful for...

✋ I am grateful for...

REFLECTIONS

🏔 I will accomplish...

👣 I need to work on...

QUALITY AND INTENSITY

	1	2	3	4	5	6	7	8	9	10
Focus And Breathing	○	○	○	○	○	○	○	○	○	○
Visions And Emotions	○	○	○	○	○	○	○	○	○	○

Malisa Salc

📅 DATE	🕐 WAKE UP

THE MORNING RITUALS

Silence	Meditation	Gratitude	Exercise	Reading
☐	☐	☐	☐	☐

THOUGHTS & INSIGHTS

I AM FEELING

GRATITUDE

✋ I am grateful for...

✋ I am grateful for...

✋ I am grateful for...

✋ I am grateful for...

✋ I am grateful for...

REFLECTIONS

⛰️ I will accomplish...

⚙️ I need to work on...

QUALITY AND INTENSITY

	Focus And Breathing	1 — 2 — 3 — 4 — 5 — 6 — 7 — 8 — 9 — 10
👁	Visions And Emotions	

THE MORNING RITUALS

Silence ☐ Meditation ☐ Gratitude ☐ Exercise ☐ Reading ☐

THOUGHTS & INSIGHTS

I AM FEELING

GRATITUDE

✋ I am grateful for...

✋ I am grateful for...

✋ I am grateful for...

✋ I am grateful for...

✋ I am grateful for...

REFLECTIONS

⛰️ I will accomplish...

🎒 I need to work on...

QUALITY AND INTENSITY

Focus And Breathing   1 — 2 — 3 — 4 — 5 — 6 — 7 — 8 — 9 — 10

👁️ Visions And Emotions

📅 DATE   🕐 WAKE UP

THE MORNING RITUALS

Silence   Meditation   Gratitude   Exercise   Reading
☐   ☐   ☐   ☐   ☐

THOUGHTS & INSIGHTS

I AM FEELING

GRATITUDE

✋ I am grateful for...

✋ I am grateful for...

✋ I am grateful for...

✋ I am grateful for...

✋ I am grateful for...

REFLECTIONS

⛰️ I will accomplish...

🏋️ I need to work on...

QUALITY AND INTENSITY

🧘 Focus And Breathing   ○   ○   ○   ○   ○   ○   ○   ○   ○   ○
                        1 —— 2 —— 3 —— 4 —— 5 —— 6 —— 7 —— 8 —— 9 —— 10
👁️ Visions And Emotions   ○   ○   ○   ○   ○   ○   ○   ○   ○   ○

📅 DATE   🕐 WAKE UP

THE MORNING RITUALS

Silence	Meditation	Gratitude	Exercise	Reading
☐	☐	☐	☐	☐

THOUGHTS & INSIGHTS

I AM FEELING

GRATITUDE

🖐 I am grateful for...

🖐 I am grateful for...

🖐 I am grateful for...

🖐 I am grateful for...

🖐 I am grateful for...

REFLECTIONS

⛰ I will accomplish...

🎯 I need to work on...

QUALITY AND INTENSITY

Focus And Breathing   1 — 2 — 3 — 4 — 5 — 6 — 7 — 8 — 9 — 10

Visions And Emotions

Malissa Salvi

📅 DATE   🕐 WAKE UP

THE MORNING RITUALS

Silence	Meditation	Gratitude	Exercise	Reading
☐	☐	☐	☐	☐

THOUGHTS & INSIGHTS

I AM FEELING

GRATITUDE

✋ I am grateful for...

✋ I am grateful for...

✋ I am grateful for...

✋ I am grateful for...

✋ I am grateful for...

REFLECTIONS

⛰️ I will accomplish...

🏋️ I need to work on...

QUALITY AND INTENSITY

Focus And Breathing   1 — 2 — 3 — 4 — 5 — 6 — 7 — 8 — 9 — 10

👁️ Visions And Emotions

📅 DATE   🕐 WAKE UP

THE MORNING RITUALS

Silence   Meditation   Gratitude   Exercise   Reading

☐   ☐   ☐   ☐   ☐

THOUGHTS & INSIGHTS

I AM FEELING

GRATITUDE

✋ I am grateful for...

✋ I am grateful for...

✋ I am grateful for...

✋ I am grateful for...

✋ I am grateful for...

REFLECTIONS

⛰️ I will accomplish...

🏋️ I need to work on...

QUALITY AND INTENSITY

	1	2	3	4	5	6	7	8	9	10
👤 Focus And Breathing	○	○	○	○	○	○	○	○	○	○
👁 Visions And Emotions	○	○	○	○	○	○	○	○	○	○

Malisa Salv

📅 DATE   🕐 WAKE UP

THE MORNING RITUALS

Silence	Meditation	Gratitude	Exercise	Reading
☐	☐	☐	☐	☐

THOUGHTS & INSIGHTS

I AM FEELING

GRATITUDE

✋ I am grateful for...

✋ I am grateful for...

✋ I am grateful for...

✋ I am grateful for...

✋ I am grateful for...

REFLECTIONS

⛰️ I will accomplish...

🔧 I need to work on...

QUALITY AND INTENSITY

👤 Focus And Breathing   1 — 2 — 3 — 4 — 5 — 6 — 7 — 8 — 9 — 10

👁️ Visions And Emotions

DATE   **WAKE UP**

THE MORNING RITUALS

Silence	Meditation	Gratitude	Exercise	Reading
☐	☐	☐	☐	☐

THOUGHTS & INSIGHTS

I AM FEELING

GRATITUDE

✋ I am grateful for...

✋ I am grateful for...

✋ I am grateful for...

✋ I am grateful for...

✋ I am grateful for...

REFLECTIONS

I will accomplish...

I need to work on...

QUALITY AND INTENSITY

Focus And Breathing   1 — 2 — 3 — 4 — 5 — 6 — 7 — 8 — 9 — 10

Visions And Emotions

Malisa Salv

📅 DATE   🕐 WAKE UP

THE MORNING RITUALS

Silence   Meditation   Gratitude   Exercise   Reading

☐   ☐   ☐   ☐   ☐

THOUGHTS & INSIGHTS

I AM FEELING

GRATITUDE

🖐 I am grateful for...

🖐 I am grateful for...

🖐 I am grateful for...

🖐 I am grateful for...

🖐 I am grateful for...

REFLECTIONS

⛰ I will accomplish...

🏋 I need to work on...

QUALITY AND INTENSITY

🧘 Focus And Breathing   1 — 2 — 3 — 4 — 5 — 6 — 7 — 8 — 9 — 10

👁 Visions And Emotions   ○   ○   ○   ○   ○   ○   ○   ○   ○   ○

THE MORNING RITUALS

Silence   Meditation   Gratitude   Exercise   Reading

☐   ☐   ☐   ☐   ☐

THOUGHTS & INSIGHTS

I AM FEELING

GRATITUDE

🖐 I am grateful for...

🖐 I am grateful for...

🖐 I am grateful for...

🖐 I am grateful for...

🖐 I am grateful for...

REFLECTIONS

⛰ I will accomplish...

🏋 I need to work on...

QUALITY AND INTENSITY

Focus And Breathing   1 — 2 — 3 — 4 — 5 — 6 — 7 — 8 — 9 — 10

Visions And Emotions

Malisa Salvi

📅 DATE   🕐 WAKE UP

THE MORNING RITUALS

Silence   Meditation   Gratitude   Exercise   Reading

☐   ☐   ☐   ☐   ☐

THOUGHTS & INSIGHTS

I AM FEELING

GRATITUDE

🖐 I am grateful for...

🖐 I am grateful for...

🖐 I am grateful for...

🖐 I am grateful for...

🖐 I am grateful for...

REFLECTIONS

⛰ I will accomplish...

👣 I need to work on...

QUALITY AND INTENSITY

Focus And Breathing   1 — 2 — 3 — 4 — 5 — 6 — 7 — 8 — 9 — 10

👁 Visions And Emotions

Malisa Salvi

📅 DATE	🕐 WAKE UP

THE MORNING RITUALS

Silence	Meditation	Gratitude	Exercise	Reading
☐	☐	☐	☐	☐

THOUGHTS & INSIGHTS

I AM FEELING

GRATITUDE

🖐 I am grateful for...

🖐 I am grateful for...

🖐 I am grateful for...

🖐 I am grateful for...

🖐 I am grateful for...

REFLECTIONS

⛰ I will accomplish...

🏅 I need to work on...

QUALITY AND INTENSITY

	1	2	3	4	5	6	7	8	9	10
👤 Focus And Breathing	○	○	○	○	○	○	○	○	○	○
👁 Visions And Emotions	○	○	○	○	○	○	○	○	○	○

Malisa Salvi

📅 DATE	🕐 WAKE UP

THE MORNING RITUALS

Silence	Meditation	Gratitude	Exercise	Reading
☐	☐	☐	☐	☐

THOUGHTS & INSIGHTS

I AM FEELING

GRATITUDE

✋ I am grateful for...

✋ I am grateful for...

✋ I am grateful for...

✋ I am grateful for...

✋ I am grateful for...

REFLECTIONS

🏔️ I will accomplish...

⚙️ I need to work on...

QUALITY AND INTENSITY

		1	2	3	4	5	6	7	8	9	10
👤 Focus And Breathing		○	○	○	○	○	○	○	○	○	○
👁️ Visions And Emotions		○	○	○	○	○	○	○	○	○	○

Malisa Salvi

THE MORNING RITUALS

Silence   Meditation   Gratitude   Exercise   Reading

☐   ☐   ☐   ☐   ☐

THOUGHTS & INSIGHTS

I AM FEELING

GRATITUDE

👋 I am grateful for...

👋 I am grateful for...

👋 I am grateful for...

👋 I am grateful for...

👋 I am grateful for...

REFLECTIONS

🏔️ I will accomplish...

🏋️ I need to work on...

QUALITY AND INTENSITY

🧘 Focus And Breathing   1 — 2 — 3 — 4 — 5 — 6 — 7 — 8 — 9 — 10

👁️ Visions And Emotions

📅 DATE   🕐 WAKE UP

THE MORNING RITUALS

Silence   Meditation   Gratitude   Exercise   Reading

☐   ☐   ☐   ☐   ☐

THOUGHTS & INSIGHTS

I AM FEELING

GRATITUDE

👋 I am grateful for...

👋 I am grateful for...

👋 I am grateful for...

👋 I am grateful for...

👋 I am grateful for...

REFLECTIONS

⛰ I will accomplish...

🏋 I need to work on...

QUALITY AND INTENSITY

Focus And Breathing

1 — 2 — 3 — 4 — 5 — 6 — 7 — 8 — 9 — 10

Visions And Emotions

📅 DATE   🕐 WAKE UP

THE MORNING RITUALS

Silence   Meditation   Gratitude   Exercise   Reading

☐   ☐   ☐   ☐   ☐

THOUGHTS & INSIGHTS

I AM FEELING

GRATITUDE

🖐 I am grateful for...

🖐 I am grateful for...

🖐 I am grateful for...

🖐 I am grateful for...

🖐 I am grateful for...

REFLECTIONS

⛰ I will accomplish...

🏋 I need to work on...

QUALITY AND INTENSITY

Focus And Breathing   1 — 2 — 3 — 4 — 5 — 6 — 7 — 8 — 9 — 10

👁 Visions And Emotions

Malisa Salvi

THE MORNING RITUALS

Silence	Meditation	Gratitude	Exercise	Reading
☐	☐	☐	☐	☐

THOUGHTS & INSIGHTS

I AM FEELING

GRATITUDE

🖐 I am grateful for...

🖐 I am grateful for...

🖐 I am grateful for...

🖐 I am grateful for...

🖐 I am grateful for...

REFLECTIONS

⛰ I will accomplish...

⚙ I need to work on...

QUALITY AND INTENSITY

	1	2	3	4	5	6	7	8	9	10
Focus And Breathing	○	○	○	○	○	○	○	○	○	○
Visions And Emotions	○	○	○	○	○	○	○	○	○	○

Malisa Salvi

THE MORNING RITUALS

Silence ☐   Meditation ☐   Gratitude ☐   Exercise ☐   Reading ☐

THOUGHTS & INSIGHTS

I AM FEELING

GRATITUDE

✋ I am grateful for...

✋ I am grateful for...

✋ I am grateful for...

✋ I am grateful for...

✋ I am grateful for...

REFLECTIONS

🏔️ I will accomplish...

🎯 I need to work on...

QUALITY AND INTENSITY

Focus And Breathing   1 — 2 — 3 — 4 — 5 — 6 — 7 — 8 — 9 — 10

Visions And Emotions

THE MORNING RITUALS

Silence	Meditation	Gratitude	Exercise	Reading
☐	☐	☐	☐	☐

THOUGHTS & INSIGHTS

I AM FEELING

GRATITUDE

👋 I am grateful for...

👋 I am grateful for...

👋 I am grateful for...

👋 I am grateful for...

👋 I am grateful for...

REFLECTIONS

⛰️ I will accomplish...

🏋️ I need to work on...

QUALITY AND INTENSITY

Focus And Breathing

Visions And Emotions

1 — 2 — 3 — 4 — 5 — 6 — 7 — 8 — 9 — 10

📅 DATE	🕐 WAKE UP

THE MORNING RITUALS

Silence	Meditation	Gratitude	Exercise	Reading
☐	☐	☐	☐	☐

THOUGHTS & INSIGHTS

I AM FEELING

GRATITUDE

✋ I am grateful for...

✋ I am grateful for...

✋ I am grateful for...

✋ I am grateful for...

✋ I am grateful for...

REFLECTIONS

⛰️ I will accomplish...

🏋️ I need to work on...

QUALITY AND INTENSITY

	1	2	3	4	5	6	7	8	9	10
🧘 Focus And Breathing										
👁️ Visions And Emotions										

Malisa Salve

📅 DATE   🕐 WAKE UP

THE MORNING RITUALS

Silence   Meditation   Gratitude   Exercise   Reading

☐   ☐   ☐   ☐   ☐

THOUGHTS & INSIGHTS

I AM FEELING

GRATITUDE

✋ I am grateful for...

✋ I am grateful for...

✋ I am grateful for...

✋ I am grateful for...

✋ I am grateful for...

REFLECTIONS

⛰️ I will accomplish...

🏋️ I need to work on...

QUALITY AND INTENSITY

🧘 Focus And Breathing   ○ ○ ○ ○ ○ ○ ○ ○ ○ ○

1 — 2 — 3 — 4 — 5 — 6 — 7 — 8 — 9 — 10

👁️ Visions And Emotions   ○ ○ ○ ○ ○ ○ ○ ○ ○ ○

Malisa Salvi

📅 **DATE**   🕐 **WAKE UP**

THE MORNING RITUALS

Silence	Meditation	Gratitude	Exercise	Reading
☐	☐	☐	☐	☐

THOUGHTS & INSIGHTS

I AM FEELING

GRATITUDE

🖐 I am grateful for...

🖐 I am grateful for...

🖐 I am grateful for...

🖐 I am grateful for...

🖐 I am grateful for...

REFLECTIONS

⛰ I will accomplish...

🏋 I need to work on...

QUALITY AND INTENSITY

Focus And Breathing   1 — 2 — 3 — 4 — 5 — 6 — 7 — 8 — 9 — 10

👁 Visions And Emotions

📅 DATE   🕐 WAKE UP

THE MORNING RITUALS

Silence   Meditation   Gratitude   Exercise   Reading
☐   ☐   ☐   ☐   ☐

THOUGHTS & INSIGHTS

I AM FEELING

GRATITUDE

✋ I am grateful for...

✋ I am grateful for...

✋ I am grateful for...

✋ I am grateful for...

✋ I am grateful for...

REFLECTIONS

⛰️ I will accomplish...

🏗️ I need to work on...

QUALITY AND INTENSITY

Focus And Breathing   ○   ○   ○   ○   ○   ○   ○   ○   ○   ○
                        1 — 2 — 3 — 4 — 5 — 6 — 7 — 8 — 9 — 10
👁️ Visions And Emotions ○   ○   ○   ○   ○   ○   ○   ○   ○   ○

📇 DATE	🕐 WAKE UP

THE MORNING RITUALS

Silence	Meditation	Gratitude	Exercise	Reading
☐	☐	☐	☐	☐

THOUGHTS & INSIGHTS

I AM FEELING

GRATITUDE

✋ I am grateful for...

✋ I am grateful for...

✋ I am grateful for...

✋ I am grateful for...

✋ I am grateful for...

REFLECTIONS

⛰ I will accomplish...

⚙ I need to work on...

QUALITY AND INTENSITY

	1	2	3	4	5	6	7	8	9	10
Focus And Breathing	○	○	○	○	○	○	○	○	○	○
Visions And Emotions	○	○	○	○	○	○	○	○	○	○

Made in the USA
Coppell, TX
21 December 2022